Feasting on Freedom

Lucas de Kretser

As always, for Rene

Contents

Foreword

Freedom has been bubbling inside me for a long time, and it is my story. Raw and honest. I've tried not to hold back. This is a story of abuse, of resilience, of growth, acceptance, and hope.

Writing this book has been one of the most rewarding experiences of my life, even if it has been hard to confront all the things that have terrified me over the past few years. Thank you so much to everyone who has been here since my first book – *A Stubborn Forest* – your support has meant the world to me and has truly been a light in the darkest times. To all my friends who have been there for me throughout the process – I couldn't have done this without you. And to those who have been there all along – I can honestly say you have kept me alive.

Freedom is finally ready. And so am I.

The End

A Haiku (Naked)

Contortionist tree,
dead – infested with Winter.
Naked and shameless.

Painting Little Devils

My sweet angel-incarnate brings me stemless pitted cherries and a fiasco of wine as the night draws on, becoming lousy and filling with the chirping of nocturnal insects.

My brush considers the empty space atop the slender neck.

'Another night alone? Another cold bed?' he asks, lingering just behind me in the golden glow of candlelight.

'I'm afraid so. Tonight – I must finish tonight,' I say, not turning away from my work.

A cold wind shrieks, and he has quit the room – retired to a chamber somewhere off through an archway to slumber under the moon. I wonder what he will dream of, if he will dream of me, or dream of somewhere else… anywhere else.

Alone now with the canvas, my eyes resume their study. I reintroduce the brush and the poplar, as I gently slide the slick bristles along the surface. I adorn it with eyebrows and take a step back to observe. No. They're not right. I decide to do away with them, tweezing so finely with the brush that soon they were never there.

His nose. His eyes. His smile. My little devil – so perfectly captured.

My luscious angel-incarnate brings me crusted bread and pitted olives, along with meats and cheeses as the sun ripens in the sky. He lingers, and gazes upon the portrait with a smile suggesting a thousand different thoughts.

'So, who is she then?'

Apricot Sky

I meet you under an apricot sky. The warm mingling of night and day above us. I must admit that you're blinding – a real man to show me how love ought to be handled.

You drive my friends away and leave me dancing under the amber-stained clouds. A lonely ballerina spinning in weathered lilac and pastel – the holes in my clothes don't bother me when I have you waiting in my bed.

I am drenched in oil, slick and sliding away from myself under a kiss of scarlet and rose. It just makes me quicker, so what if I can't grip the ground? You say I don't need to stay anywhere for too long anyway.

You strike the match, and I can't help but catch, and turn this twilight into a spectacle of flame. *You are so wild, so full of fire* – you whisper in my ear. I rest my head on your shoulder as you take me softly to Bedlam.

May Morning

Slept on your mother's couch.
Crept into the jarring sunlight
of an early May morning.

The sky a painful blue dapple.
Candy-floss constellations
suspended in Heaven.

Your words echo in my head:
you never drink,
you're no fun!

The sun has melted just there on the pavement –
a bulbous orange bleeding
amber curls into muddy puddles.

My head is quaking.
I drank so much
to kick up a racket for you.

Ivory walls sway to Arlo Parks.
Baby leaves dance to the tune
and blow away with the breeze.

You left me in the kitchen,
swinging back and forth,
unsure of my feet.

I find you sleeping behind curtains.
A ghostly glow peeking in
where the fabrics kiss.

I clean up your sick
as you nurse your hangover
and I nurse mine.

Somewhere to Write

I wake in the night.
Carefully reach over him
for my little leather-bound book
to write in the dim kitchen light.

Perching at the window:
I envy the trees across the street
as they turn honey gold,
as they shed their leaves
like old moth-eaten coats.

I'll have to write something for them.

It's late and my eyes are exhausted.
The Asam tea still warms my lungs.
His head lolls to one side.
He is so calm when he dreams.
I'd boil the kettle for another tea…
but I dare not wake him.

Valentine's Day

We've been apart for a few days,
and each one has hurt more than the last.
Our bed is empty and cold,
and I know I'll have to start calling it mine again.

My bed.
My home.
My life.

I met you when I was eighteen,
just on the precipice.
You knew your life a little better than I...
thought you'd figured everything out.

But I came and changed all that.
We uprooted each other,
tore down each other's safety,
so we could build our own home.

But these days I can't see you.
We live parallel lives in this little city.
I count the days 'til I can see you again,
'til I can tell you I forgive you.

Come Out, Mr. Wolf

Weaving between the pines: a peculiar sketch. A shifting cloud with a long black snout.

'Come out, Mr. Wolf!' I call. 'Why must you linger in the trees? It seems so dark in your woods, have you drawn a great veil over the sun?'

I break the treeline. Your ghostly shadow stalks me from within a thicket.

'Where are your, Mr. Wolf?' I cry. 'Are you watching me? Your branches are heavy with snow, was it you who brought this blizzard? What did you use to prod the clouds and cause them to let out such a great sigh of snow?'

I wander through your winter-scape. Ice-rivers. Frost-flowers. Vanilla-grass. Ivory-trees.

'Do you see, Mr. Wolf,' I ask, 'how beautiful your home is? I've strayed very far from the path… might I steal an apple from your orchard? Or better yet, a kiss from your snowberry lips?'

Heavy yet graceful paws tread the frozen earth. Your hawk-like eyes focus on me.

'Please, Mr. Wolf,' I beg, 'can I stay here with you? If not, then my bed is soft and warm. Shall I take you there? Shall I let you slip under the sheets with me?'

You announce yourself. Muscled legs. A maw of wicked teeth. A coat of grey wire.

'There you are, Mr. Wolf,' I sigh, 'such beauty… I'm so very cold, would you permit me to snuggle into your fur? Would you carry me away in those gentle jaws?'

Swimming in His Gut

I have been swallowed up,
I have been utterly devoured.
Swimming, drowning in his gut,
sinking, losing all my power.

I used to love laughter, but now
I don't think it sounds like me.
He makes me forget to grieve,
he makes me forget to breathe.

I see a ghost in the mirror,
I see nothing of me in there.
The soul has vacated the body,
the spirit has made room for you.

I have vanished into you,
I have become a memory of smoke.
Your coldness has bled into me,
your complacency has been adopted.

Existing in a sack of bones
that I do not own.
You have given me a key
but it does not fit the lock.

Maya,

I know now why the caged bird sings.
Your turmoil is incomparable to mine
because this is a cage of my own design.
But I'm certain we sing the same song –
a stifled warbling,
bleak and maudlin.

We have the need to sing of ourselves,
not for ego or for vanity
but to remind ourselves
that we even exist.

We are driven by the need to be heard.
To drink in the clouds and breathe
our whispers into violent screams
that soar into the sky,
until we are as inescapable as the air
and our vocal cords tear.

Virgin Sighs

I still see you
past the trees and the brush,
past the wild and untamed flowers,
beyond the ever-climbing ivy.

Peeking through
the wall of green lace like a bride
gazing through her veil
on the best day of her life.

Innocent eyes
behind brambles and thorns.

Virgin sighs
behind the coming storms.

Poor, beautiful fool
wearing your cap of bells so well.
Everyone is laughing
but you're not in on this joke.

It's all at your expense:
the wedding, the honeymoon,
her pale dress. But you don't know
it's your name on the bill.

Bleeding green
underneath your gorgeous gown.

Loathsome scheme
beneath a wrinkled frown.

Dinner for Jackals

Remember how I gave you the shirt off my back, and in turn you snapped my spine?

You abandoned me in the mud. A feast for scavengers. It was the insects first, running over me and shouldering their way under my skin. Teeth slicing. Miniscule mandibles.

Thunderbirds circled as the snow began to fall. They swooped down from the milky clouds and dug their talons into me, tearing through the muscle, rummaging through the red for anything of value.

The vultures took off with a squawk when the jackals came. Haphazardly lolloping across the plain with their broken feet. I noted their eyes of burning bourbon as they ripped off my arms. I noted their maws – curled in crooked smiles – as they went to work on my legs.

They stuffed their stomachs until they were fit to burst, then rammed their paws down their throats and vomited up everything they had swallowed. As they demanded more, you appeared as if from nowhere, and flipped me onto my stomach so they could wriggle their snouts under my ribs and sniff out the last pieces of me that remained.

A mangled corpse in the Winter sun – a scattering of bleached bones come the Summer rain.

A Portrait of July

The air in the café
was fragrant and thick
with lemon and coffee.

> Guests arrived at eight.
> We looked so good together,
> everyone said so.

Sweet Summer berries
decorate the wild hedgerow,
waiting to be plucked.

> Raise another glass
> for these two sweet boys of ours!
> Mark your calendars.

A slow conversation
beside Callow Grove
provided direction.

> The restaurant lights
> kept up their glow 'til midnight
> when the party died.

Something has got to change.
Boys should kiss gently,
not with amethyst lips.

> My bed so wide and cold.
> No imprint of you.
> I am so sick of Summer.

If I Don't Go Now

Three years in:
you promise daily, the drinking will stop
but the bottles keep piling up.
I have to pull you out of a tight spot
every Friday night at a run-down bar.
The bailiffs knock down our door one day,
calling on your debts.
Now they're on my head, and mine to pay.

Twelve years in:
gathered here for New Year's Eve,
celebrating the end of the '20's,
when my mother comes up to me,
'didn't you wanna *be* something?
Didn't you wanna *do* something?'
'Perhaps once…
But I gave it all up for him.'

Fifteen years in:
I have forgotten my name.
You are bored of your job, and you drink,
into sweet oblivion every day.
I learn to drive in secret,
taking lessons when you're at the office.
But you find the paper-trail
and slash my tires.

If I don't go now, I'll never go.

Twenty years in:
my friends beg me to leave you
when I turn up to lunch
with another broken arm.
They arrange another intervention.

But their phone calls can't reach
all the way to Tokyo
where you have taken me.

If I don't go now, I'll never go.
If I don't go now, I'll never go.

You Can Keep the River

I float down-river.
Banks green with wild garlic,
waters blue as the sky.
The sky: peeking through the arches of the viaduct
and packed into perfect sapphire windows.

The wind kisses the river.
Its chill runs deep in me.
Was I born in its depths?
Its depths that I might call home before long,
if I'm not wary of the changing tide.

This river is a liar.
It does not flow into any sea
but crashes off the end of the earth.
The earth that was promised to me,
that I know now I shall never receive.

That Down House

A sea of softly swaying grass
surrounds an island of a house.
Weathered grey walls.
Sunken pale steps
ascending to a rotting
wooden porch.
Stained windows.
An emaciated horse
out front
kicking at the dirt.

The gables –
mazes for mice.
The walls –
towers for termites.
The beams –
sanctuaries for spiders.
The boards –
racetracks for rats.
The hearth –
a bolthole for bats.

There is a suitcase
propping open the front door,
waiting for vicious winds
to blow in
and break this breaking house.
The buckles are breathing,
constricting and expanding.
Fresh boots,
apples and tonics,
a map of the mountains.

A wash of white-wailing grass
eats away at the island house.
Crumbling grey walls.
Haggard, forsaken steps
descending from the rotten
woodworm porch.
Shattered windows.
An emaciated horse
lifts its head
for its rider.

Feasting on Freedom

A Haiku (Blood of Sunshine)

A yellow field
drip-feeds the blood of sunshine.
Tree begins to thaw.

He Speaks

He speaks to his moon,
imploring his love to remain in the sky,
to not plunge into the ocean
however tempting the blue might seem.

She is the Summer song;
the gentle sweeping sand,
the veridian grass seeping
onto a golden canvas.

He sounds like you do.
Although he doesn't have the accent
that carried down the phone
for six sweet months.

He reminds me of Greece
where we walked. The statues
you pointed out to me
beneath the hot Athenian sun.

His piano keys take me back
to long bus rides. To wasted time.
To nights spent in vineyards
typing out messages, just to delete them.

He told me so much would change
but my love would remain the same.
He was right: I still have a fondness
for a boy who never existed.

Vermilion

You are every shade of Mother Earth.
Vermilion and streaks of straw,
ebony hair pressed from the dirt.

Roses bloom for you when you caress them just right,
and clouds part at the mere suggestion
that you might desire a little more sunlight.

Apiaries abundant with honey at your behest,
dolphins gliding over the waves,
lions waltzing to impress.

This whole world dances to your tune.
It breaks its back time after time,
begging that you'll approve.

You're setting fire to the cornfields;
morphing nightmares into reality
with a snap of your fingers.

All that love and adoration
and boundless, unending devotion
and you are blind to it.

Summer on the Lawn

Caught the 8.55 into town, then the 9.20 to the garden centre. Called you a dozen times. No answer.

Spent the day juggling tea and coffee; bubbling, boiling, spitting, hissing customers. At four, I cleaned down and made the 4.05.

Called you when I boarded; tried 'til I disembarked. Walked home as the buses roasted in the sun.

Made food quickly. Ate in the garden. Kicked the ball around for the dog.

Took a bath listening to Lana in the sunset.

You text: *still at work. Will call later.*

I missed your midnight call: I was in Toussaint, wine drunk.

Gorgeous Busker

Took shelter from the sun
on the Stacks.
Listened to a gorgeous busker
singing something that meant nothing,
about coffee mornings and broken bones.

The sound filled the square
and bounced off the churches and the bars.
Then became so small and tender
like a child's cry
caught in his throat.

The Severn

I remember how we used to sit
beside the river waiting for ships.
I remember the days by the Severn,
hot and tired, waiting for Heaven.

Adopted dreams,
bastard boys disguised as monstrous men.
Our loves tore us apart.
We slept next to each other like alley cats.
When I landed behind bars,
I scribbled down my escape plan
and fashioned a battleship.
Sent it sailing through the sewers to you.

I remember the day the river
burst its banks and flooded the town.
I remember the trees on the outcrop
that collapsed into the rush.

We were so young,
we lived in each other's pockets
and wandered down long white corridors,
ate in quaint cafes,
cried about our first jobs,
played at being grown-ups,
for two years
until I moved away.

I last saw you by the river.
We sat under the sun. We argued.
I left you there as it swelled
and walked home past the river in the road.

It feels so strange not to talk to you

but it feels so good to breathe.
I heard the news through friends
and it made me so angry
that you might have a shot at happiness
while I was knee-deep in agony.
Today, I read that your girl had been born
and it made me smile.

In Summer, I'll come and sit
beside the river and wait for ships.
Spend a day by the Severn,
hot and tired, still in pursuit of Heaven.

'We'll get some more stuff from the car,' mum says. 'Make the bed while we're gone?'

The bed in question: a wooden frame on wheels, coated in coarse blue fuzz, topped with an ill-fitted mattress. My sheets are perched in the bottom corner in a neat pile of black and white, and muted beige. In the corner, the duvet oozes out of a freshly opened suitcase.

I fish my speaker from my backpack and turn the music up in a desperate attempt to bring a sense of 'home' to this alien space. But the music does little to soften the harsh edges of the faded white walls, or to brighten the grey wash of sky outside the window. Forgetting the bed, I inspect every corner of the room, wondering if I can sleep here every night for a year, all alone.

The ensuite: a shower with a dreary curtain; a horribly pockmarked floor that I partly cover with my fresh bathmat; an impossibly clean toilet and sink; a counter which seems to swallow up my little green washbag. I miss my bathroom at home, where the wooden floor is warm, and the bathtub's underside is painted green, and sweet lavender diffuses on the windowsill.

The door swings open.

'You haven't made the bed yet!' mum jokes, holding two more boxes in her arms.

'Yeah… I'll do it in a bit. I don't know where to start.'

These boxes contain my whole life. Every book and vinyl; one bowl; spoon; fork; knife; mug; a pair of chopsticks; a cactus-shaped glass. I remember standing among them, hugging my parents, and almost telling them to pack everything back into the van and take me back home; but I must not have said anything, because they left and did not take me with them.

With the new silence, new emptiness creeps in – barren draws, a bare shelf, a space where a wardrobe should go, a mirror that shows me how out of place I look. I haul my TV and XBOX onto the desk and plug in the extension cable, before adding my laptop to this mess of wires. Finally, I slide a forbidden wax-burner into the corner. After outfitting my snack drawer and displaying my vinyl collection atop the unit, I decide I've done enough unpacking for the time being. Now comes the task of making new friends…

From my room, the corridor curves like a wave back to the landing where another family emerge from the lift, hauling their own luggage. Walking through a door to my left, I am presented with a long row of rooms. One is open, and I catch a glimpse of two girls chatting; I think they see me too, but I'm too awkward to go in. I stumble to the dead-end of the corridor and stare out of the window.

I could call mum and dad right now. Tell them it's all too much, and this place is too alien, and too scary, and it's never going to feel like home.

But I can't. I need to last a day at least.

I breathe deeply and turn. Go to the room…

I pop my head in and say 'hi'.

The Rose Room / Four Walls

Still awake at 2. Fire alarm.
My eyes are bloodshot again.
The moon peering in. Light fog.
I pour my tenth coffee.

Night drifts slowly by. Moon dipping.
Silver light shines and dulls.
I greet a young sun. 'Morning,
I was up first,' I taunt.

She messages at 10. 'You up?'
Her room smells like lemon.
I ease with her laugh. Deep blue.
Leaving, the calm does too.

I spray vanilla. Windows open.
The old sun falls away.
I shower again. Fifth time.
The cold lashes at my legs.

'Come over in 5?'. 'Yeah, coming.'
I run the corridor.
Cotton and cold now. Crisp air.
The smell of a new home.

I speak until 2. Mostly smiles.
She listens, then speaks 'til 3.
After 3, I cry. Freely.
She just holds me tighter.

Her eyes lull at 5. I slip out.
My white room seems hostile.
Caged in all around. Four walls.
Just me – bad company.

Drowning in this sea. Misery.
Everything is debris.
I reach out for her. Clinging.
If I ever let go…

A little kick-drum. A small jolt.
Some breath in me again.
It's only fleeting. Stevie's gift.
She's always been there.

The slowest crooning. So soothing.
Oozing like sweet honey.
Caressing my brain. Cooling me.
Brings me to sleep at last.

The Water Goes

We should climb through this window
and venture into the vivid sunset.
There is enough pigment there to stain us all.
Deep cobalt for our sadness,
fire-orange for our endless hope.

The night seems to have been built for us.
Rapturous and wonderful,
glistening with unbridled freedom.
The early moon tugs at the earth as it threatens
to sever gravity and become a wayward comet.

We slide into the fountain, before the blood-smear sky.
The watercolours have bled into the pool
where they bubble and furiously fry.
Perfect violet is tangled in my hair,
the water goes deep fuchsia.

The Blue Smoke

The Blue Smoke. A seedy bar. Dimly lit.
Bustling with trysts and affairs and underhand dealings.
There is a piano with dusty keys and a singer
whose voice is gravelly… bitter like the whiskey
the men drink, splashed over slick, slimy rocks
to pluck up the courage to reach over
and smack the ass of the closest boy.
I spy you in a booth, cloaked in shadow,
but I would know your face anywhere. So sharp and angular,
gaunt – that's what mum said when I showed her
who I was bringing home that December.

I pay. Drink up. Leave the bar.
My phone comes alive. Buzz. Buzz. Buzz.
It's you. *Was that you in the bar, in the Blue Smoke?*
Might have been – I say.
Really, do you want company?
I roll my eyes, then wonder… do I?
I'm staying nearby. The hotel just over the road.
Come to my room? I miss you…
You miss me? Where was this longing four years ago,
when I was devoted to you so completely?
I did love you, I did care, but I messed it up.
You did. And as desperately as I desire company tonight,
I won't let you back into my head to fester
or into my bed to play.

In the next bar, a New-York-style dive,
I examine the bartender. He seems familiar

as he throws metal shakers and pirouettes
as they flip, before catching them.
Biology or physics. Certainly, he reminds me
of school. Of classrooms. Pens and paper.
Only when he turns to me, and asks what I'm drinking,
and his eyes connect with mine, do I recognize him…

Underneath the Pier

You were still staining my lips as I walked away.
Left you fumbling at your belt beneath the pier,
the waves lapping at your boots.

I wondered: was my mouth wetter and warmer
than every girl at school you chose over me?
I decided: yes.

I bet they never made you tremble like that.
The way I bit… your legs shook
as I dug my nails deep into your thighs.

You unloaded on my tongue in a minute.
Stared into my eyes like I owned every inch
and in that moment, I almost shared your pleasure.

When I was a boy, I craved you:
you were quick and smart,
and your fingers could work wonders on me.

The first time I slipped into myself,
I thought of the outline I saw in your shorts
and the fists that once graced my cheek.

As I touched myself, I screamed your name:
did you taste like strawberries?
Would you feel like fire inside me?

Tonight, your fingers tugged at my hair
but it was brutish and careless.
You tasted like every other boy.

I went home and stared at myself in the mirror:

Ruffled hair and soaked knees.
I felt nothing,
but you'd unloaded your stress for the night.

The Wine in My Glass

The wine in my glass is white and sharp.
The light from the lounge leaks into the bedroom
but there is no restless soul there for it to disturb.
Outside, the wind moans like the ghosts on my screen.
If sober, I'd be curled under a blanket,
peeping over the top just as I did when I was a child.
The shadows in here dress like monstrous beasts
and flood the white walls in a sea of coal.
I sit in revelry like an audience, sipping wine
and observing this laughable shadow-show.
I should take myself to bed…
but this wine is good, and I want more.
I pour another glass.
Then another.
So many boys in my phone…
but you do not respond to me. I
shouldn't be wanting right now, I
should be happy to sleep alone.
But I'm *never* satisfied.
The wanting *never* lets me go.
I hear neighbours
bouncing to bed,
it's 2,
or so the clock says.
Time
for company.

Falling into Morning

I sit in my chair. Watch the sky
while I wait.
Moon falls through stars.
Slides through the firmament.
Skidding skater.
You buzz the flat. I let you in.
Find you on the stairs.
Wrapped up against the cold.
I'd ask your name if I cared –
I don't.

I take you to my room.
Offer you a drink. You pass.
Take off your coat. Then your shirt.
Your trousers. Pants.
You show yourself off.
I eye it. Consider it.
Am I startled?
Am I scared?
No.

Arms like steel.
Legs of muscle.
Sinew tearing bone.
Snap my back,
back into place.
Have me like that.
Any way you want.

Take what I have to give,
it's not a lot.

But it's all I have left.
Sleep. Stay the night.
Don't go.
I can't abide an empty bed.

And when you drift
down that way
I sizzle like
an electric fault
and make excuses.

Take what I have to give,
it's not a lot.
But it's all I have left.
From all the thieves who've taken.
Taken.
Taken.
Taken.

Sleep.
Stay the night.
Don't go.
I can't abide an empty bed.

A Little Longer in the Sun

They are so small.
Like specks of turmeric dust
that have been snapped at by flytraps
as they have floated from the kitchen window.
Like the smallest koi fish
that have somehow swum
from the pond to the tree.

They would make very little jam,
these miniscule tigers
without claws or stripes,
without jaws or eyes.
These distant sunrises
hooked, but loosely held
on the ends of fishing rods.

I will let my tangerines ripen
a little longer in the sun.
Let these suggestions of amber,
these whispers of citrine
drink in the sun
and grow ripe. Grow fat.
Grow.

The Morning

Industrial Sea

Watching the clouds skipping and prancing.
Drifting through the sky like smoke off the industrial
sea.
I greet the morning with hot chai tea
to purge the taste of the night from my tongue.

The sun is a pale disk slowly rolling,
creeping in from the corner of my window.
It's Summer blaze, now a Winter flicker. Freshly
plucked
from slumber like a lily slid from the earth.

She appears more like her nocturnal sister today
and darts behind a shifting hill of pallid smoke,
and the world mourns her vanishing. But she returns
darkened and diminished – but still, the sun.

Sicilian Marmalade

My breakfast table is busy:
Sicilian marmalade is scraped onto toast
and my fruit bowl is heavy with lemons and limes
and my mug is piping hot with coffee
and my robins sing morning trills to me.

Oozing honey is stirred three times
and my candle-flame bobs playfully
and my incense cracks and smoulders
and my robins sing morning trills to me.

Breadcrumbs

My best friend started talking to you.

'He's hot – your type.'

I thought you seemed clever, like someone I could connect with. But you only had eyes for her, and she burned for you until she grew bored and doused the flames.

But I still burn.

Another year, another friend wanted you.

'He remembers you… the *cute* one.'

Are these breadcrumbs you're leaving me, or are you just messy? She paraded the idea of you before me every day for a week, and then she found another boy.

I still think of you.

Cold Winter birthed, and I saw you again.

'It's been years… I haven't forgotten about you.'

That's what I would have said, if you'd noticed me standing there like a fool in the doorway – waiting for you to beckon me over or even remember my face.

I still dream of you, hoping the breadcrumbs – trailing through fields of snow and over turbulent oceans – will lead to you, lounging in the glow of a fire, reading some old book, and asking 'what took you so long?'

But I fear… I'll just find you by Fair Sabrina, tearing off chunks of bread to throw to squabbling ducks.

Night Wanderings

Along the canal, my first love took in the cool air. He wore the jacket I'd bought him two years ago, but I still made him shiver.

I gazed into the restaurant where my best friend worked. She stood smiling – listening the specials – and suddenly glanced at the door. I'd gone.

Mum and dad, reading in separate chairs. Dad's cigarette sparkling in the ashtray. Mum's glasses almost sliding off the end of her nose. Marigold eyes noted my presence at the window, and I fled.

The same routines every night.

I returned to my grave as the sun spilled out.

Willow

I waited beneath the willow as Halley burned up in the sky. Her whispery lustre trailed between islands of starlight that illuminated the delicate field of reeds I had wandered through to reach our tree.

Pacing back and forth, I scanned the perimeter for movement, peering through the willow's curtain of greying green and lacey blue.

The crickets chirped; the glow-worms decorated the mammoth trunk; the toads croaked in their shallow ponds; the dwarf spiders spun themselves homes in the leaves.

I waited.

Halley slipped from view; her light bled into the moonglow and fell away.

I waited.

Elizabeth in Her Bath of Reeds

Her loose amber hair clung to her bare back; clammy and cold.

'How did you find this place?' asked the girl who sat on the bank, dipping her toes in the glassy water.

'A witch brought me here; claimed it was magic.' Elizabeth laughed. 'And maybe it is… it gives me the one thing that all the Kings and Dukes of Europe cannot hope to offer.'

'And what is that?' her young friend enquired.

'Peace. Aren't you coming in?'

The girl clutched her silks to cover her body, hesitating.

'Won't they see?' she bleated.

Elizabeth rose slightly out of the water, exposing the tops of her pale breasts. The treeline cracked, and twigs snapped in chorus. But the Lady shouted 'begone' and the footsteps shuffled away from the clearing.

'If you feel their eyes on you, I'll have their heads. Come for a swim. You deserve peace as much as I do.'

Great Green Appalachia

In the Appalachian Mountains, I discovered a little hamlet. Just a dozen houses growing out of the green, swaying on stilts rooted in the grey under-rock.

Bloated veins reached out from the weary city in the deep valley; and here, from the seldom-used station, slender, unstopped arteries extended further to smaller villages deeper in the wild.

I rented a single room – from June, a sweet old thing. Spent a week in her garden, sketching the tulip trees and the Indian bats in the vibrant moonlight.

Even as copperheads coiled about my ankles, I kept my eyes always on the wide-open sky.

Bookshop

He came to a stop outside a bookshop, and in the glass's cold reflection he adjusted the frayed coat that let the wind in through its tears. Behind the window lived a golden light, an array of shelves and books, smiling faces and bold titles, warm eyes flecked with thoughtful snow. Of all the doorways… this seemed the most magical corner he had seen in town.

He could sleep in that doorway – a strangely enchanting place to slumber – in the glow of the window display, with literature's greatest to keep him company 'til the morning.

In his dreams, he lives amongst that display, on the other side of the glass, in the warmth of the store, under the eyes of loving readers, his skin the pages under their caring hands.

In the darkest times, he leans upon Emily Bronte for support, and goes to Oscar Wilde when his opium addiction flares. In nights of all-encompassing sadness, he might drink into the morning with Sylvia Plath. And when the winter is unbearable, he visits his friend Daniel Defoe, and sleeps on the beaches.

Far from the snow that this late in the night, turns to grey sludge.

Scar in the Clouds

I love the stillness of the night.
How the white lights emit a stale glow.

For a second the world has frozen,
creeping slowly
ever so slowly
forward.

The scar in the clouds
cradles the moon.

How cruel of it to remind me
of how I once
used to cradle
you.

The bars are bustling with life
but out here there is no sound.

I am the only one sober.
The only one
walking slowly
home.

You would always drink in there
when we would fight.

The bar with the red door,
the blue door,
white door,
door.

The scar in the clouds

cradles the moon.

The World is So Loud

I hear you come whistling down the street – a strange old tune I've not heard for years. I'm almost overtaken by the urge to hide behind my curtain as you pass beneath my frosted window. But I quickly get the impression that you are not here for me, and so your eyes will not drift so high as to spot me at the glass.

The image of Sherlock Holmes, in that long black trench coat, weaving through the fog puddles like dry ice blanketing the cobbles. Your woolly cap could be mistaken for a jet-black top hat in this blur – and you would tip it in respect to the coffin that you might march before, steadying yourself on your silver-topped cane, the top of which shines like a diamond in the dark. If it's not a cane, then it must be an umbrella; one you'll unfurl at any second when the snow begins to spiral down from the bulging clouds, and waltz about in the leisurely downpour – thinking this quaint little alley in England is the glittering main street in Paris, and this easy-falling snow is a rainstorm.

Wreathed in mist and fog; the bringer of ground-scraping clouds. They dance about your feet, pouring out of your boots and creeping into every corner of the street, yet they do not rise above your shins because that way you would not be able to see. Unable to hold myself back, I force my window all the way open. I call out to you. Although you do not look up, you halt in your tracks. The mist thickens; it rises and boils and bubbles like molten strawberry jam, and you slip beneath the soup.

I slide into my boots, wrap up in my scarf and gloves, and dash into the street to search for you. I find only an umbrella shivering on the road, clawed at by wisps of a once-heavy fog. The coldness of the ivory handle burns even through the gloves; the little black strap is easily undone.

Then, the clouds sigh out a slow-rush of snowflakes, and I open your umbrella, and try to recall the steps of your snow-dance.

Este

'Ms Bennet?' a timid little voice came through the phone.

'Might be,' Este replied. 'Who's this?'

'It's Laurence Taylor, I wanted to -'

'Oh God,' she cut him off. 'How'd you get this number?'

'Your agent.'

'Well, look at him going behind my back...' Este tipped her cigarette back and forth between her fingers. 'So, what do you want?'

'I wanted to know if you'd read my script yet?'

'I read it tonight in-fact.'

'And?'

'You're a great writer. I'd love to take the part...'

'Oh! Ms Bennet that's -'

'If it was a play. You know I don't do film.'

'Ms Bennet please – this part is perfect for you. Can't you see yourself in Martha's shoes?'

'I could. On the boards.'

There was a silence on the line.

'The studio is willing to pay handsomely for your time, Ms Bennet.'

Este placed a cigarette between her lips and inhaled so deeply that her lungs fogged up like the morning coast.

'A hundred thousand dollars.'

She opened her mouth in a sharp gasp and choked on the smoke. It billowed out of her in a great plume as if she were a dragon. Este pressed the cigarette into the ashtray balanced on the arm of her chair.

'Well… maybe it's time to try film after all.'

Back in this Body

I am infested with the men I have been with:
jammed in my throat
rammed between my legs
planted in my skull.
I have a kiss on my lips
I have a grip on my waist.
When I try to reach my fingertips
I am met with an insurmountable resistance.

Translucent, tissue-skin.
My soul swims beneath.
A presence boils behind
bloodshot, blue, and grey eyes.
This body – old, haunted house
is a detriment to me –
it fights me at every turn.
I need an exorcism – I call a priest.

My veins are flushed with holy water
to see if you'll drown, but you swim.
I am peeled open; fire is poured inside.
You emerge after nuclear winter,
but with this rebirth you seem thinner.
You are stretched. You are tearing.
I am here to win back this body
limb by treacherous limb.
My soul is expanding, and soon
there will be no room left for you.

Something Beautiful

Once I was too full of pain,
I pushed out the wolf's leg
and snapped shut like a bear trap.
Maybe you'll come to understand why
I retreated to the edge of life
and sat amongst bloody leaves.

I lay down and you unravel me,
ease me gently open,
unpick me like King's tapestry.
There is a stopper in your throat
preventing your soul from pouring
into me when you kiss me.

How do I already trust you?
I thought it would be years
before I let someone in again.
If we take this slow,
moving like barges in the night,
we could have something truly beautiful on our hands.

Still a Child

If I must be shapeless and empty
to be filled with your love
then let my body grow fat and let me starve.

If I am fated to blaze like a wildfire,
to reach the gates of Heaven and aspire higher,
then let the smoke roll in and let me expire.

If I long for sparrows to decorate the dawn,
but awaken always to a cold and empty morning,
then I suppose I can wait as long as it takes.

If I am sentenced to sentences of silence
punctuated with moments of pleasure and danger,
then I suppose that would be just fine.

If I'm ashamed of myself, curse my reflection,
grow destructive, and lose all sense of direction,
then I suppose that's alright – I'm still a child.

It's Been Long Enough

I go forth into the grove
to find the one with branches so heavy
that the fruits can almost kiss the ground,
that even the terriers can almost reach them
with no more than a skip and a hop.

Dangling lightbulbs.
Fat globules of marmalade.
Sun-spheres of fire
to clasp in my hands,
leaving no scorch marks.

It's been long enough.
I sever a dozen or two
from the tree,
leaving enough for another day,
and drop them into my basket.

In the kitchen, I stand making jam.
The fruit convulse in the raging water,
their peel melting and losing all shape
as their segments ripple and tear.
They are battered and dislodged
by pounds of sugar, that spit and dissolve,
leaving a bubbling sea in the pan.
Brilliant and peppered with fiery crescents.
I have never seen something as beautiful
as the jam in this pan.

I would like to plant more trees,
grow more fruit and make more jam.

Figs… I like the sound of figs.

Afterword

Thank you to the editors of Pandora's Inbox in which the following pieces have appeared: 'Great Green Appalachia', 'Willow' and 'The World is So Loud'.

Thank you to the editors of The Drabble in which the following piece has appeared: 'Somewhere to Write'.

Feasting on Freedom is the sophomore collection by author Lucas de Kretser, composed of forty-four carefully selected poems and short stories to reflect the author's personal journey over the past few years.

Acknowledgments

Thank you to my marvellous illustrator, Claudia Gambles for designing the cover with me, and for being a great friend along the way.

Thank you to all those who have supported me over the past few years – you know who you are. This book has been a labour of love and of pain, and it would never have been possible without so many people to lean on, and so many shoulders to cry on.

About the Author

Lucas de Kretser is a creative writing student, author of poetry and flash fiction, and terrible parody fanfiction that shall forever be hidden.

This is de Kretser's second collection, and a follow-up to 2021's *A Stubborn Forest*. More of his work can be found on his Instagram @lucasdekretser and on his website: Lucasdekretser.wordpress.com